Before there were trucks and tractors...

They Did It With Horses

Before there were trucks and tractors...

They Did It With Horses

A Scrapbook of Photos from
the Philip Weber Collection

Heart Prairie Press

Copyright ©2000 by Heart Prairie Press

All rights reserved. No part of this publication may be reproduced or transmitted in any form, by any means, electronic or mechanical, including photocopy, recording, or any information storage and retrieval system without the written permission of the Publisher.

Publisher's Cataloging-inPublication

Weber, Philip.
    Before there were trucks and tractors--they
    did it with horses: a scrapbook of photos from
    the Philip Weber Collection / [Philip Weber]. --
    1st ed.
        p. cm.
    ISBN: 1-882199-05-7

    1. Horses--Transportation--Pirctorial works.
2. Horses--Transportation--History. 3. Horse-drawn
vehicles--Pictorial works. 4. Horse-drawn
vehicles--History. 5. Draft horses--Pictorial works.
6. Draft horses--history. I. Title.
    SF285.385.W43 2000   636.15'0222
                             I00-448

Front Cover: As pretty as a picture, an American Express Company outfit, fine horses, shiny harness, and a tip-top wagon they can be proud of. 1918. *American Railway Express Co.*

Back Cover: In downtown Elyria, Ohio, the Andress Carriage and Harness Shop also maintained a livery stable in its first floor. In addition to selling carriages (seen in the top window with a statue of a horse) and harness items (seeen in the lower right window), the shop also sold bicycles. *Author's Collection.*

Dedication

This book is dedicated to the memory of Wayne Dinsmore, past secretary of the Horse and Mule Association of America. A tireless champion of the workhorse, Dinsmore promoted the use of conventional horsepower in place of the rapidly developing truck and tractor power.

Formed in the early 1920s the Horse & Mule Association was funded by a wide variety of interested businesses including saddlery and harness makers, light and heavy horse breeders, horseshoe and horseshoe nail manufacturers, and farriers, among others. It touted the economic advantages of using horses and mules over trucks and tractors by publishing hundreds of leaflets targeted at specific types of businesses such as dairies, retail coal dealers, farmers, construction firms and moving companies. In addition, Dinsmore wrote hundreds of columns and guest editorials in many of the trade magazines and newspapers of the day.

The following excerpt from the May/June 1938 issue of *Teamwork* (published by the U.S. Hame Company) serves as an excellent example of Dinsmore's promotional style:

> "I make just as much as my neighbors who use tractors, and I save a great deal more."
>
> This terse comment by an Indiana farmer, sums up the present horse versus tractor situation.
>
> Thinking farmers, who want to get out of debt, who desire to improve the fertility of their farms, and who appreciate the cash income resulting from raising their own replacements so that one or two of the older animals can be sold each year, are using horses or mules—and they know they are "saving a great deal more."

Another example of Dinsmore's crusade to stem the tide of truck and tractor power can be found on pages 22 and 23 of this book where we reproduce a portion of a pamphlet where he tries to convince dairy companies to return to horsedrawn delivery wagons.

It would be easy to dismiss Dinsmore's crusade as Quixotic and sentimental. It was exactly the opposite. He never sentimentalized horsepower, but touted its benefits in a purely practical, pragmatic sense. Many of his arguments are still sound today, a half century later.

Acknowledgements

The photographs in this book have been acquired from many sources. A partial list includes:

Norman Coughlin
Laurence Dedrick
C.P. Fox
Huber Gullaugh
Bob Lomas
Robert Mischka

John R. Miller
Laurent Rottiers
Frits van Solt
Dick Sparrow
Lee Weatherly

The author gratefully acknowledges the contributions made by these individuals and by those who have been inadvertently omitted from this list.

Table of Contents

Chapter	Page
1. Dairies and Bakeries	.2
2. Working in the Woods	.32
3. Building America	.50
4. Fire Fighting	.68
5. Moving the Freight	.82
6. Moving People	122
7. Circus Horses	142
8. From Brewery to Bar	158
9. Daily Deliveries	170
10. Agriculture	206
11. Public Performance	228
12. Street Scenes	248

About the Author

Philip Weber was born in Cleveland, Ohio, August 26, 1913. When he was seventeen years old, Phil left his job as a camera operator with the Rapid Copy Service to work in his father's wholesale grocery business called Weber's Fruit & Vegetable Company.

The company had been started years earlier by Phil's father, Henry, and a partner, Morris Weinstein. Earlier, Morris had traded in the firm's horse and wagon for a truck. When Morris died a few years after that, Henry sold the truck and returned to using a horse and wagon for deliveries because he had never driven the truck and was reluctant to learn how.

Philip Weber on his last delivery horse, Lindy, in 1939, outside his stable.

That horse, Charley, was the first of four that Phil used in the business from 1930 until 1940 when he sold the business and took a job as a punch press operator at National Screw Manufacturers. He worked for National Screw for the next 33 years before retiring in the early 1970s.

He was good at his job, receiving several awards for suggesting ways to improve productivity in the plant. He and his wife, Verna, raised three children.

Philip Weber

"Other than doing my job, and taking care of my family, my favorite thing to do was to look at horses," Phil said. "My interest in horses has never waned. I love to be around them, in the barn, smelling the leather and hay."

Although he was never to own another horse himself, Phil immersed himself in horses in other ways. He began collecting photographs and drawings of horses, writing to companies that used horses and asking for copies of any photos they might have showing their horses in action.

He would send 50 postcards at a time to various firms. Boxes of their replies provide testimony to Philip's diligent pursuit of photographs. Many of these photographs showed up in various horse magazines published in the U.S. "Phil Weber's Scrapbook" became a regular feature in many magazines.

Today, the apartment Phil shares with his second wife, Corine, is crammed with horse memorabilia. Phil is a human card catalog for these artifacts, and likes nothing more than to dig through the piles of photos and reminisce about the way that horses used to do the work which is now being done by trucks and tractors.

One: Dairies and Bakeries

Chapter 1-Dairies and Bakeries

This Schlukebur delivery wagon could bring you a wide variety of goods, provided the sale was made in cash. Here it is parked on South Ebert Street in St. Paul, Minnesota in June 1906. *Minnesota Historical Society Photo. George Lucas Collection.*

They Did It With Horses

Right: This man delivered baked goods in 1896. *Ontario Archives.*

Below: This unit was making retail deliveries of milk from "tubercullin tested" dairy cows in Clinton County, Indiana, in 1925. A lighter rig such as this one would often make deliveries in the rural areas, being able to cover more ground in a day than the larger, heavier vehicles used in the city. *J.C. Allen Photo.*

Chapter 1-Dairies and Bakeries

They Did It With Horses

These two staged photos illustrate the transition in milk delivery from the neck yoke buckets, to the push cart with one large container and dipper, to the horsedrawn cart and finally to the rubber-tired horsedrawn wagon. The deliverymen are dressed in period uniforms and the dairy's name is prominent in each example. *Author's Collection.*

Chapter 1-Dairies and Bakeries

The Bowman Dairy Company was the largest dairy in Chicago when this picture was taken in 1928. Here we see a fleet of 24 horsedrawn wagons strung out in front of the dairy building, easily outnumbering their motorized counterparts parked alongside. This photo had been previously retouched for some reason, with the name of the dairy changed from Bowman to Bowmar, perhaps to avoid copyright infringement. *National Dairy Council Photo.*

During World War II, Dean Dairy returned to using horses to deliver milk to save gasoline and rubber. They showed their horses to success at local fairs as well. *Author's Collection.*

They Did It With Horses

Most milk delivery wagons were drop center, side-entry. Here are two shots of rear-entry wagons used in Cleveland, Ohio, in the early 1940s. *Author's Collection.*

Chapter 1-Dairies and Bakeries

Horses were sharp shod for winter service. This shot of a Oshkosh, WIsconsin, dairy deliveryman in 1951 includes an example of cream-top bottles. The specially-designed bottles allowed the customer to put a spoon or ladle inside the top of the bottle to hold back the milk when pouring off the cream. *Author's Collection.*

This Detroit dairy operated for Sealtest Foods, Inc., through the 1940s. *Spencer & Wychoff Photo.*

They Did It With Horses

Here is one of the 650 horses owned by the Belle Vernon Dairy in Cleveland, Ohio, in 1936. The harness has plenty of nickel plating and the collar sports a scotch housing. *Author's Collection.*

This Wanzer & Sons Dairy wagon is an example of the type used by many dairies in 1935 when this photo was taken. It did not have a drop center, because the flat floor would provide easier access while the wagon was loaded at the docks. *Author's Collection.*

Chapter 1-Dairies and Bakeries

During World War II, many gas-powered trucks were converted to horsedrawn wagons. This truck, built in 1930, was pulled by a horse in Chicago in 1942. *Author's Collection.*

Several Midwestern divisions of the Beatrice Creamery used horsedrawn milk delivery wagons in the 1950s. This unit operated in Mattoon, Illinois, in 1952. *Author's Collection.*

They Did It With Horses

Above: An entry in the annual Work Horse Parade in London, England in 1954. *Photo by A. Hustwitt.*

Left: Price's Dairy of Hazelton, Pennsylvania, was the last American dairy to use horses on a regular dairy route. This photo was taken in 1972. *Author's Photo.*

Chapter 1-Dairies and Bakeries

This was one of the last horse drawn wagons used by Tellings Belle Vernon in Cleveland to make wholesale deliveries in the downtown area in 1941. Originally pulled by teams of horses, these wagons were later handled by a single horse in shafts, as the company begain using larger Belgian horses. *Author's Collection.*

They Did It With Horses

Chapter 1-Dairies and Bakeries

In 1935, this outfit was used more for competitions at local horse shows, fairs and parades than for hauling dairy products. *Author's Collection.*

15

They Did It With Horses

This Meadow Gold wagon delivered to St. Louis stores and restaurants in 1945. *Author's Collection.*

The Gridley Dairy made home deliveries during the winter of 1926 in Milwaukee. *Author's Collection.*

Chapter 1-Dairies and Bakeries

Delivering milk to Chicago apartments in 1945. *Author's Collection.*

These seven Belgian geldings were among a stable of over 600 horses owned by Tellings Belle Vernon Dairy Co., in Cleveland, Ohio, in 1936. The Dairy kept four stables throughout Cleveland. The milk came in on railroad cars in large cans. Large wagons pulled by three horses brought these milk cans to the Dairy where it was bottled individually and sent out in delivery wagons. *Krohn Studios Photo.*

They Did It With Horses

Chapter 1-Dairies and Bakeries

Above: This wagon is of the type used by many dairies for milk deliveries. *Author's Collection.*

Left: This photo shows a lovely turnout in Belfast, New York. Undated. *Photo courtesy of Laurence Dedrick.*

They Did It With Horses

Above: Larger, wholesale delivery wagons were often pulled by a team instead of a single horse. The wagon above is also fitted with a brake that the driver operated with the handle on the side of the wagon. Milwaukee, 1941. *Charles Philip Fox Collection.*

Right: The Silverwood Dairy of Edmonton, Alberta, Canada, used this large Percheron to pull one of its delivery wagons in 1956. The horse stands with its ears pointed back to listen for the driver's commands. Note the braided mane complete with flowers. *Author's Collection.*

Chapter 1-Dairies and Bakeries

Top: Beatrice Creamery delivered with wagons like these in Galesburg, Illinois, in June of 1945.

Center: Crowley's Milk Co. of Binghamton, New York, in 1937 had wagons with solid rubber tires and ball-bearing wheels.

Left: The driver had to step up pretty far to to get into this wagon. Chicago, 1926.

Author's Collection Photos.

They Did It With Horses

Horses save from $30,000 to $50,000 in the delivery of every million dollars worth of milk.

Among the facts developed—fully substantiated by closely kept records—was that, by and large, depending upon the territory in which the comparisons were made, the delivery of a million dollars' worth of milk by horse and wagon costs from $30,000 to $50,000 **less** than by motor truck. That makes a good starting point for what follows. It is well for the reader—if it is still of the opinion that "modern conditions" demand motor equipment exclusively—to remember the foregoing basic truth. To the concern acquainted with million dollar sales, the savings figure will strike home with force. A **saving** of that size is enough to command the interest of the largest milk company. Those whose turnover is of less magnitude may easily compute what **their** savings would be if horses were more generally used.

Common Sense Speaks

Leaving figures aside for the moment, let us draw upon plain common sense — which tells you that a good horse following the milk salesman as he makes his rounds, stopping when commanded and jogging on to the next house at a word—is the most economical means of making house-to-house milk deliveries.

It is expensive to stop and start a motor, and time-killing for the driver to leave his truck, cover a block or more, and then walk back to his vehicle only to repeat the process. The horse-drawn wagon **keeps up** with the driver and enables him to cover his route much more quickly.

Again, the salesman on a horse route has a better chance to win new customers than the motor route man, because he can spend more time on his route without the expense of a running motor, or frequent stops, with less equipment depreciation, and with shorter walking trips between customers and vehicle.

The wagon salesman can keep a closer watch for new families moving into the neighborhood; can see his customers more frequently; can step up his sales per family; can sell more of other items to present milk buyers; can keep a better look-out for the dissatisfied customers of other customers of other companies covering the same territory.

The wagon driver, then, with more time for selling—less time for walking back and forth—more time

with his customers when needed—becomes a more productive employee and therefore a better money-maker. This point is easily arrived at, because a trained horse soon becomes automatic in action—requires little driving after the first few steps—soon memorizes the stops and turns—and becomes almost human in the way he covers the route with his driver.

From 85 to 95 percent of truck delivery time—from first to last stop—is spent by the salesman in traveling on foot from vehicle to customer or from one customer to the next. By cutting down this time, the horse-drawn vehicle becomes the money-saver which statistics prove it to be.

Horse-Drawn Vehicles More Quiet

Vicious propaganda has been put out in an effort to make milk buyers believe that horse-drawn vehicles are noiser than trucks. But according to exhaustive tests made by impartial investigators, a steel-shod horse, drawing a steel-tired wagon, makes an average noise—when passing a microphone—that is only twice the regular street noises, while the average noise of a gasoline truck is two and a half times regular street noises.

The truck is started in low gear, then shifted through. Everyone understands, and detests, that noise. The truck makes frequent stops and starts. Such a process makes a noise that is sharp and penetrating. On the other hand, the noise of horse and vehicle, traveling at ordinary house-to-house gait, is more regular and even —less disturbing—less jarring on sensitive nerves.

Discontent among unthinking milk customers has been deliberately aroused for the sole purpose of discouraging horse deliveries in favor of motor. Without realizing the facts, housewives have been agitated even to the point of boycott and some milk companies, fearing the results of such propoganda, have motorized their fleets against their better judgement.

But if any person—dealer or customer— will only give this matter a second thought, he will see that the claim of greater quietness for the motor vehicle is not only ill-founded, but that the horse-drawn vehicle makes a materially better showing in this respect.

Above and Next Page: Excerpts from a 1940 Horse and Mule Association of America booklet.

Chapter 1-Dairies and Bakeries

A modern type delivery unit equipped with pneumatic tires Maintenance costs on wagons thus equipped are very low. Draft is light, even with low wheels and noise is greatly minimized.

TABLE NO. 1

HORSE EXPENSE   Per Route Per Month

Depreciation	$ 1.61
Feed	13.75
Bedding	.88
Shoeing	4.10
Stable Supplies	.05
Veterinary and Medicine	.29
Stable Wages	7.15
Stable Rent	9.47
TOTAL	$37.30

WAGON EXPENSE

Depreciation	$4.08
Repairs	3.99
Repair Wages	.17
Supplies	.96
License	.42
TOTAL	$9.62

HARNESS EXPENSE

Depreciation	$ .42
Repairs	.36
Repair Wages	.41
Supplies	.24
TOTAL	$1.43
Total Horse, Wagon and Harness Expense	$48.35
Sales per month per one horse route	$1,155.22
Delivery cost per dollar of sales	.0418

TABLE NO. 2

GASOLINE TRUCK   441 Gasoline truck routes
                               Per Route Per Month

Depreciation	$21.72
Gas and Oil	19.24
Insurance	5.13
License	2.37
Repairs and Supplies	16.19
Tires	3.47
Repair Wages	3.99
Upkeep Wages	4.75
Garage Rent	7.32
TOTAL	$84.18
Sales per truck route per month	$1,024.73
Delivery cost per dollar of sales	.0821

TABLE NO. 3

ELECTRIC TRUCK   96 Electric truck routes
                               Per Route Per Month

Electric Charger Depreciation	$3.56
Electric Charger Repairs	1.42
Electric Truck Upkeep Wages	7.86
Electricity Charge	17.84
Electric Truck Depreciation	27.19
License and Insurance	5.97
Electric Truck Repairs	8.83
Supplies and Miscellaneous	1.37
Tire Depreciation	1.79
Garage Rent	7.18
Battery Depreciation	6.08
TOTAL	$89.09
Sales per truck route per month	$1,060.02
Delivery cost per dollar of sales	.084

They Did It With Horses

Above: The John Guedelhoefer Wagon Company of Indianapolis, Indiana, and the De Kalb Wagon Company of De Kalb, Illinois, specialized in making drop center delivery wagons for many of the dairies at that time. *Author's Collection.*

Right: "Eat a Plate of Ice Cream Every Day" urges the sign under the roof of the Moores & Ross Milk Co. wagon in Columbus, Ohio, in 1946. *Author's Collection.*

Chapter 1-Dairies and Bakeries

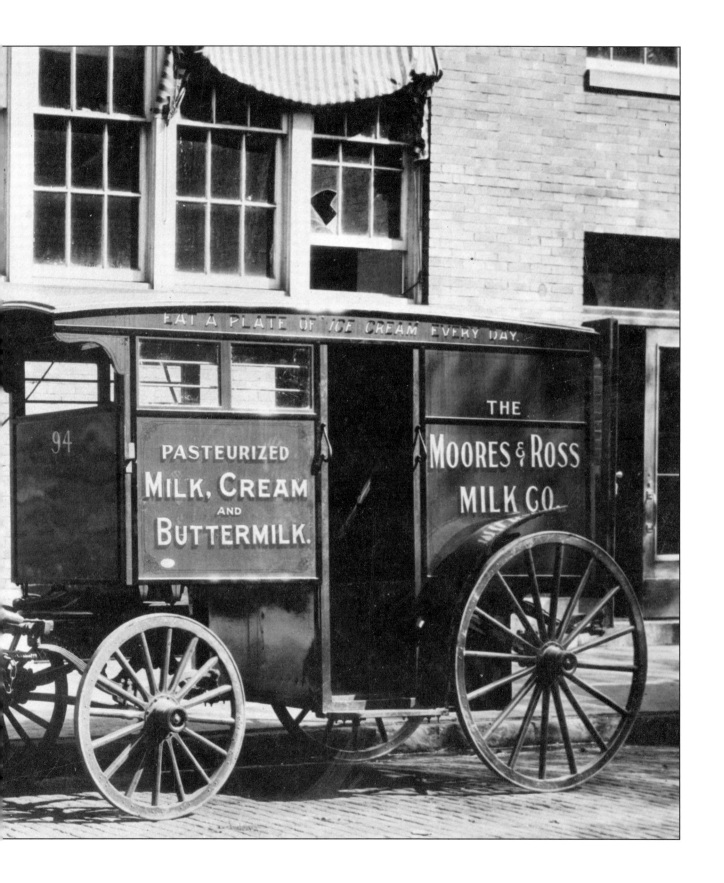

They Did It With Horses

A Horsedrawn bakery delivery wagon working the streets of Windsor, Ontario, Canada in 1944. *Author's Collection.*

A retail bakery wagon delivering fresh baked goods to the customer's door in Toronto, Canada, in the 1930s. *Author's Collection.*

Chapter 1-Dairies and Bakeries

Danas Brothers Baking Company of Akron, Ohio, delivered their goods with this wagon and team in 1926. Because bread tended to be bulky and not heavy, most bakery delivery wagons were pulled by just one horse. Perhaps this wagon was used for hauling flour. *Author's Collection.*

This wagon is an example of what a number of bakeries used for home delivery. Buffalo, New York, 1947. *Author's Collection.*

They Did It With Horses

Chapter 1-Dairies and Bakeries

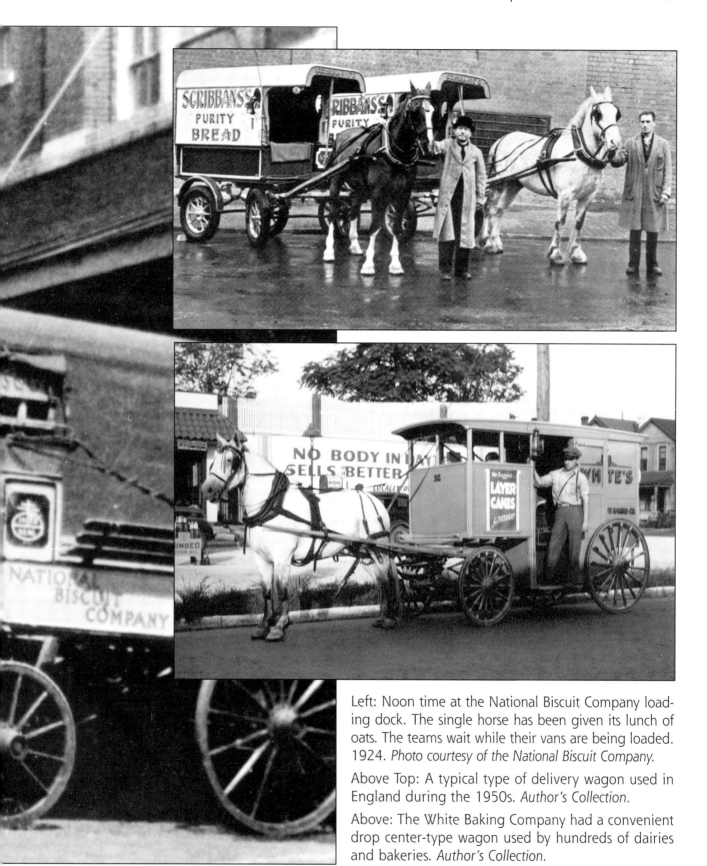

Left: Noon time at the National Biscuit Company loading dock. The single horse has been given its lunch of oats. The teams wait while their vans are being loaded. 1924. *Photo courtesy of the National Biscuit Company.*

Above Top: A typical type of delivery wagon used in England during the 1950s. *Author's Collection.*

Above: The White Baking Company had a convenient drop center-type wagon used by hundreds of dairies and bakeries. *Author's Collection.*

They Did It With Horses

Chapter 1-Dairies and Bakeries

Left: A horse and its driver pull into the dairy stable on a cold, snowy day. *Charles Philip Fox Photo.*

Top: A baker's driver and horse in 1918. *Author's Collection.*

Above: A very practical delivery wagon owned by Christy Bread in Toronto, Canada, in 1904. *Author's Collection.*

Two: Working in the Woods

Chapter 2-Working in the Woods

This virgin stand of hardwoods in Michigan was being logged on a large scale with over 70 men and teams of horses in 1900. Three men stand on the log being lifted by the steam engine. *Author's Collection.*

They Did It With Horses

Above: a large log being pulled by a team on a Miamisburg, Ohio, street in 1904. *Author's Collection.*

Right: A long line of drivers and their horse teams wait with their large loads of logs for their turn at the sawmill. 1916. *U.S. Forest Service Photo.*

Chapter 2-Working in the Woods

They Did It With Horses

Chapter 2-Working in the Woods

Top: Giant wheels moving an underslung log at the Californian Lassen National Forest in 1918. The left wheel horse is saddled as well as harnessed, with the logger riding as well as driving the hitch.

The large wheels were placed so they straddled the log, just ahead of the log's center The pole was pointed upward, bringing the bolster behind the axle down to where it was chained to the log. Then when the pole was pulled down, the front end of the log was lifted off the ground. *E.S. Shipp Photo.*

Left: Hauling logs, underslung to the high wheels at the Coconina National Forest in Arizona in 1910. These oversized wheels were made in Manistee, Michigan. *National Forest Service Photo.*

They Did It With Horses

Hauling a load of red pine lumber from the forest in the Sault Ste. Marie district of Ontario, Canada, in 1956. *Photo Courtesy of Province of Ontario Department of Lands and Forests.*

Chapter 2-Working in the Woods

Hauling Ponderosa Pine logs from the National Forest to the sawmills in New Mexico in 1924. *Photo Courtesy of U.S. Forest Service.*

The teamster driving these horses is all but hidden by the dust coming up on the off side of the horses. He was hauling logs in 1942 in western Australia. *Australian News & Information Bureau Photo.*

They Did It With Horses

Chapter 2-Working in the Woods

Top: Horses pulling a load out of British Columbia, Canada, woods in 1912. *Photo courtesy of K.E. Brown.*

Left: A good view of the equipment and men that, along with the horses, played a vital role in the timber boom of the early 1900s. *U.S. Forest Service Photo.*

They Did It With Horses

A good sized load for this four horse team in Minnesota. *Forest History Society Photo.*

Two sleds of logs were joined for this load pulled by six horses. Loggers would ice the tracks where the sled runners traveled to make the going easier for the horses. *U.S. Forest Service Photo*

Chapter 2-Working in the Woods

Moving the timber on a cold morning in Michigan in 1914. *Author's Collection.*

43

They Did It With Horses

Chapter 2-Working in the Woods

Logging in Red Gut Bay of Rainey Lake in Ontario, Canada, in 1905. *Province of Ontario Department of Lands & Forests Photo.*

They Did It With Horses

Chapter 2-Working in the Woods

These loggers are removing the mature trees but allowing the young trees to remain, ensuring a crop of timber for the next generation. *U.S. Photo Service Photo.*

They Did It With Horses

The men and horses that worked in the P. Kelly Lumber Company posed for a photo near Galloway, Alberta, in 1911. *A. Downey Photo.*

Chapter 2-Working in the Woods

Three: Building America

Chapter 3-Building America

This 1906 crew of the Southern New England Telephone Company take a moment to pose for the camera. This group has apparently enlisted the help of a dog, perched up on the pole, and a goat, leashed and held on the ground below. The near horse is adorned with a plume in its bridle and sports a bell from its yoke strap. The small cart behind the group is used to haul the tall poles behind the wagon. *Southern New England Telephone Co. Photo.*

They Did It With Horses

Above: It took a lot of horses to dig the basement for St. Luke's Catholic Church in Hopkinton, Iowa, in 1910. *Author's Collection.*

Right: This Marathon Oil Company crew went out to work in the middle of winter in Findlay, Ohio, in 1915. *Marathon Oil Co. Photo.*

Chapter 3-Building America

They Did It With Horses

They used large, heavy machinery to harvest the oil from America's oil-rich Ohio valley. But before they could use the machinery, they had to get it to the well site. The horses, sixteen in all, were hooked in sets of four. The eveners were chained to a log which, in turn, was chained directly to the massive wagon carrying the oil rig. 1912. *Author's Collection.*

At least sixteen horses can be seen here to move a piece of oil drilling equipment near Bartlesville, Oklahoma, in 1914. The two horses seen at the far left of the photo appear to be straining as they help steady the load, their chain running directly back to the top of the machinery. The other horses are being placed in position. An oil well can be seen in the distance above the second team from the left. *Author's Collection.*

Chapter 3-Building America

55

They Did It With Horses

Chapter 3-Building America

Top Left: This tool wagon for the Philadelphia Electric Company was pulled by a team of dapple gray Percherons in 1916. *Author's Collection.*

Above: A Bell Telephone of Canada construction gang poses with townspeople at Clifford, Ontario, Canada, in 1912. *Author's Collection.*

They Did It With Horses

Chapter 3-Building America

Above: This crew built and maintained telephone lines in Ohio in 1916. The young girl on the wagon was probably the daughter of one of the crew members. *Ohio Belle Telephone Company Photo.*

Left: This underground "trouble crew" worked for the Illuminating Company in 1904. *Author's Collection.*

They Did It With Horses

Chapter 3-Building America

Top Left: Ready Construction Company used these drop-bottom dump wagons to excavate building sites in Chicago. 1912. *Norman Coughlin Photo.*

Above: A drop-bottom dump wagon used by the Wilmette, Illinois, street department in 1910. *Wilmette Historical Museum Photo.*

Left: The Ready Construction Company of Chicago, Illinois, had these teams in their service in 1922. The man driving the dump wagon on the right is dressed more for the office than for hauling dirt at a construction site. *Norm Coughlin Photo.*

They Did It With Horses

Chapter 3-Building America

Left: A load of explosives is being carried up the road where it will be used to blast open fissures in solid, petroleum-bearing rock. 1906. At first, gunpowder was used to provide the charge. Later, nitroglycerine was substituted. *Drake Well Museum Photo.*

Below: A team stands ready to pull its load of nitroglycerine used to help drill oil wells. 1908. *American Petroleum Institute Photo.*

63

They Did It With Horses

Above: This type of dump wagon was very practical for moving sand, gravel and dirt. *Author's Collection*.

Chapter 3-Building America

Left: A large iron turbine was hauled for the Columbia Gas Company by horses in 1900 near Pittsburgh. Notice the wide-rimmed wheels and the man alert at the brake to stop the load if needed. *Author's Collection.*

Below: Eighteen horses and six men made up this road crew which operated an elevator-loader to grade the land for the Grand Trunk Pacific Railway in Alberta, Canada. The elevator's cutting disc loosened the soil which was carried up a large conveyor into dump wagons which drove in a continuous circle around the loader. *Author's Collection.*

They Did It With Horses

Chapter 3-Building America

Above: Excavating using horses and Fresno scrapers. 1933. Cleveland. *Author's Collection.*

Opposite Page: Teamsters and their horses hauling out the refuse from the underground work at the Pennsylvania Railway Tunnel in 1909 New York City. *Author's Collection.*

67

Four: Fire Fighting

The Cleveland, Ohio, fire department made its last run of this horsedrawn hose wagon on April 17, 1922. *Sunday Plain Dealer.*

Chapter 4-Fire Fighting

They Did It With Horses

70

Chapter 4-Fire Fighting

Above: Hitching and harnessing up in a hurry. 1902. *Kansas City Fire Department Photo.*

Left: Tall and leggy, these horses were well-built to pull fire engines for the Cleveland, Ohio, fire department. *Cleveland Public Library Photo.*

Above: A beautiful team of Percherons pulled this Cleveland, Ohio, fire department hook and ladder wagon in 1910. *Author's Collection.*

Right: An engine and hose wagon in front of Chicago Engine House no. 40 in 1905. *Chicago Historical Society Photo.*

Chapter 5-Moving the Freight

They Did It With Horses

Chapter 5-Moving the Freight

Above: London (England) Cooperative Society's general purpose utility wagon, 1957. *Author's Collection.*

Left: Lumber wagons drawn by horses and mules. *Author's Collection*

91

They Did It With Horses

Chapter 5-Moving the Freight

Above: F. J. Trautmann, a butter, egg and cheese merchant, had a very reliable means to serve his customers—namely a sturdy and patient horse. Buffalo, New York, 1912. *Author's Collection.*

Left: A fine example of the type of wagon used by many merchants. 1918. *Author's Collection.*

They Did It With Horses

This Chicago-area moving firm had a variety of horsedrawn wagons. 1925. *Author's Collection.*

Lamertons of London (England) entered this four-up in the Van Horse Parade in 1956. *A Hustwitt Photo.*

Chapter 5-Moving the Freight

A good example of the horses used commercially at the time. Chicago, 1923. *Norman Coughlin Collection.*

Bess and Bill are the fine team in this photograph taken in Seattle in 1907. *Author's Collection.*

They Did It With Horses

Above: Libby, McNeill and Libby's loading dock in Chicago in 1906. Notice the fine quality of horses that they used. *Author's Collection.*

Right: A brewery's delivery driver and local cop ham it up for the camera. *Author's Collection.*

Chapter 5-Moving the Freight

They Did It With Horses

Chapter 5-Moving the Freight

The horse farm at Cornell University in Ithaca, New York, kept this crew of well-equipped teams in 1913. *Laurence Deidrik Photo.*

They Did It With Horses

Chapter 5-Moving the Freight

These teamsters and their hitches delivered for the W.J. Transfer Company in Nome, Alaska, in 1907. *Bettman Archives Photo.*

They Did It With Horses

Above: This team, owned by Lasham Cartage Company, Chicago, won the pulling contest at the County Fair in the Chicago Stadium. *Author's Collection.*

Outside a paper and cardboard company, a young man fills buckets to water the firm's fleet of horses. New York City, 1924. *Norman Coughlin Collection.*

Chapter 5-Moving the Freight

103

They Did It With Horses

The unit above calls itself a "Scenery Waggon", while the one at top right is labeled a "Scene Truck". Both were long narrow vehicles that could carry a great weight of lumber. 1906. *Provincial Archives of Alberta, E. Brown Collection.*

Chapter 5-Moving the Freight

89

They Did It With Horses

Chapter 5-Moving the Freight

Above: London (England) Cooperative Society's general purpose utility wagon, 1957. *Author's Collection.*

Left: Lumber wagons drawn by horses and mules. *Author's Collection*

91

They Did It With Horses

Chapter 5-Moving the Freight

Above: F. J. Trautmann, a butter, egg and cheese merchant, had a very reliable means to serve his customers—namely a sturdy and patient horse. Buffalo, New York, 1912. *Author's Collection.*

Left: A fine example of the type of wagon used by many merchants. 1918. *Author's Collection.*

They Did It With Horses

This Chicago-area moving firm had a variety of horsedrawn wagons. 1925. *Author's Collection.*

Lamertons of London (England) entered this four-up in the Van Horse Parade in 1956. *A Hustwitt Photo.*

Chapter 5-Moving the Freight

A good example of the horses used commercially at the time. Chicago, 1923. *Norman Coughlin Collection.*

Bess and Bill are the fine team in this photograph taken in Seattle in 1907. *Author's Collection.*

They Did It With Horses

Above: Libby, McNeill and Libby's loading dock in Chicago in 1906. Notice the fine quality of horses that they used. *Author's Collection.*

Right: A brewery's delivery driver and local cop ham it up for the camera. *Author's Collection.*

Chapter 5-Moving the Freight

They Did It With Horses

Chapter 5-Moving the Freight

The horse farm at Cornell University in Ithaca, New York, kept this crew of well-equipped teams in 1913. *Laurence Deidrik Photo.*

They Did It With Horses

Chapter 5-Moving the Freight

These teamsters and their hitches delivered for the W.J. Transfer Company in Nome, Alaska, in 1907. *Bettman Archives Photo.*

They Did It With Horses

Above: This team, owned by Lasham Cartage Company, Chicago, won the pulling contest at the County Fair in the Chicago Stadium. *Author's Collection.*

Outside a paper and cardboard company, a young man fills buckets to water the firm's fleet of horses. New York City, 1924. *Norman Coughlin Collection.*

Chapter 5-Moving the Freight

They Did It With Horses

The unit above calls itself a "Scenery Waggon", while the one at top right is labeled a "Scene Truck". Both were long narrow vehicles that could carry a great weight of lumber. 1906. *Provincial Archives of Alberta, E. Brown Collection.*

Chapter 5-Moving the Freight

105

They Did It With Horses

Above: These large, well-put-together horses worked for the Dawson Transfer Company in the Yukon Territory in 1910. *Public Archives of Canada.*

Right Top: This young man, parked below a "No Parking Sign" is holding the reins on one of the cartage wagons of the Canadian National Express Company in Toronto, Ontario, in 1923. *Charles Stevens Photo.*

Right Bottom: In 1946 New York City, these rather large vans were drawn by a single horse. *Author Photo.*

Chapter 5-Moving the Freight

They Did It With Horses

Montgomery Ward used this horsedrawn wagon to make its deliveries in the 1890s in Chicago. *Chicago Historical Society Photo.*

Chapter 5-Moving the Freight

109

They Did It With Horses

Cornell University owned these horses and hitched them to a coal wagon on its Ithaca, New York, campus in 1907. *Laurence Dedrick Photo (Laurence's grandfather is driving).*

Chapter 5-Moving the Freight

Top: J.C. Ritchie, of Stratford, Iowa, showed several fine entries at the local fairs in the 1920s. Here he exhibits a hitch of roan colored Belgians in 1921. *Author's Collection.*

Bottom: The neck yoke on this New England truck harness connected direct to the breeching with the backup straps to provide better backing power with this stake body dray cartage wagon in 1900 Portland, Maine. *Author's Collection.*

111

They Did It With Horses

The city of Cleveland erected this arch in its public square as part of its centennial celebration in 1876. *Cleveland Public Library Photo.*

Chapter 5-Moving the Freight

They Did It With Horses

The Johnson Moving Company of Denver, Colorado, used these two units in 1912. *Author's Collection.*

Chapter 5-Moving the Freight

115

They Did It With Horses

Above: The Pacific Cartage Company has a nice turnout as this photo shows. Calgary, Alberta, 1902. *Glenbow Historical Society Photo.*

Above: The Western News Co. worked their show horses and showed their work horses. This team won first place for work horse teams at the 1923 Chicago International Horse Show. *Author's Collection.*

Chapter 5-Moving the Freight

117

They Did It With Horses

Above: This 1920 Cleveland Ohio photo shows a heavy dray used for cartage at the time. *Author's Collection.*

Right: Chicago is a city well known for its commercial activity. At the time this photo was taken it depended largely on heavy drays like this one. 1916. *The Chicago Historical Society.*

Below: This Dayton, Ohio, moving van was well built, roomy and nicely decorated. 1910. *Huber Gillaugh Collection.*

118

Chapter 5-Moving the Freight

They Did It With Horses

Above: This tank wagon hauled the crude oil from the Pennsylvanian oil fields to the refinery in 1900. *Author's Collection.*

Top Right: Oil from the tanks in the background was drip-pumped into the wagon in the foreground. The driver could raise the canapy of his wagon in case of bad weather. Baltimore, 1916. *American Petroleum Institute Photo.*

Right: When Standard Oil Company introduced its first tank wagons, harnesss shops were still big business on main street. Columbus, Kansas. *Author's Collection.*

Chapter 5-Moving the Freight

Six: Moving People

Chapter 6-Moving People

Coaches and other vehicles, all loaded with sightseers, pause at a vista on Skyline Parkway in Duluth, Minnesota, in 1911. *Author's Collection.*

123

They Did It With Horses

Above: This two-wheeled cart called the "caleche" was the prevailing vehicle in the province of Quebec, Canada around 1916. *Author's Collection.*

One of the most mis-used terms when discussing horsedrawn vehicles is the hansom cab. The vehicle at right is a true hansom cab, with the driver sitting at the rear and over the top of a two-wheeled cart. 1898. *Author's Collection.*

Chapter 6-Moving People

They Did It With Horses

Chapter 6-Moving People

Above: This roof seat break was pulled by four handsome horses and carried six finely-dressed passengers in 1905 Cleveland, Ohio. *Author's Collection.*

Left: This family of five took their turnout to the park for a Sunday afternoon drive in Duluth, Minnesota, in 1910. *Author's Collection.*

They Did It With Horses

Right: Tourists pause for a photo on the rim of the Grand Canyon in 1903. *Santa Fe Railway Photo.*

Chapter 6-Moving People

Left: A coach loaded with cargo and passengers travels overland in Western Canada. This unit featured well-conditioned horses, a durable vehicle and a talented driver. *Canadian Pacific Railroad.*

Chapter 6-Moving People

Opposite Page Top and Above: This proud team of horses was used by the Dean of Cornell University in 1908. *Courtesy of Lawrence Dedrick.*

Opposite Page Bottom: This passenger wagon was used in Tucson, Arizona, and had a fringe on top and roll-down curtains on the sides in back. 1880. *Author's Collection.*

They Did It With Horses

Right: A load of tourists are being taken to their hotel from the railroad depot on a large stage pulled by six matching horses. The hotel is likely one of the buildings in the background with the balconies facing the street. Cascade Mountain, Banff, Canada, 1914. *Byron Harmon Photo.*

Below: A group of railroad passengers prepare to leave the restaurant where they stopped for a meal, perhaps to return to the train and continue on their journey. *Author's Collection.*

Chapter 6-Moving People

They Did It With Horses

Tally-Ho on Granville St. Vancouver, B.C.
Sept. 20" 1907

Chapter 6-Moving People

Clockwise from Top Left: A coaching party at Yellowstone National Park in 1898; a group ready to start on a coach drive in 1913 Bermuda; a four-in-hand taking tourists from their Hotel in Pacific Grove, California, circa 1900; and a Tally-Ho in downtown Vancouver, British Colombia, Canada, in 1907. *Author's Collection.*

They Did It With Horses

To commemorate the advances made in transportation, the 1933 Century of Progress Fair in Chicago featured this photo of "How they went to the World's Fair in 1893." *Ontario Archives.*

Chapter 6-Moving People

137

They Did It With Horses

W.H. Horton Livery Stable at the corner of Kirk Avenue and Henry Street in Roanoke, Virginia, in 1895. *Norfolk & Western Railroad Photo.*

Chapter 6-Moving People

They Did It With Horses

Right: A hotel omnibus in front of the shop where it was built. 1892. *Author's Collection.*

Below: Road or mail coach originally used in England in the latter part of the 19th century. *Circus World Museum Photo.*

Bottom: An excellent example of the fine art of coach making of earlier days. *H.S. Crocker Co. Photo.*

Chapter 6-Moving People

141

Seven: Circus Horses

Chapter 7-Circus Horses

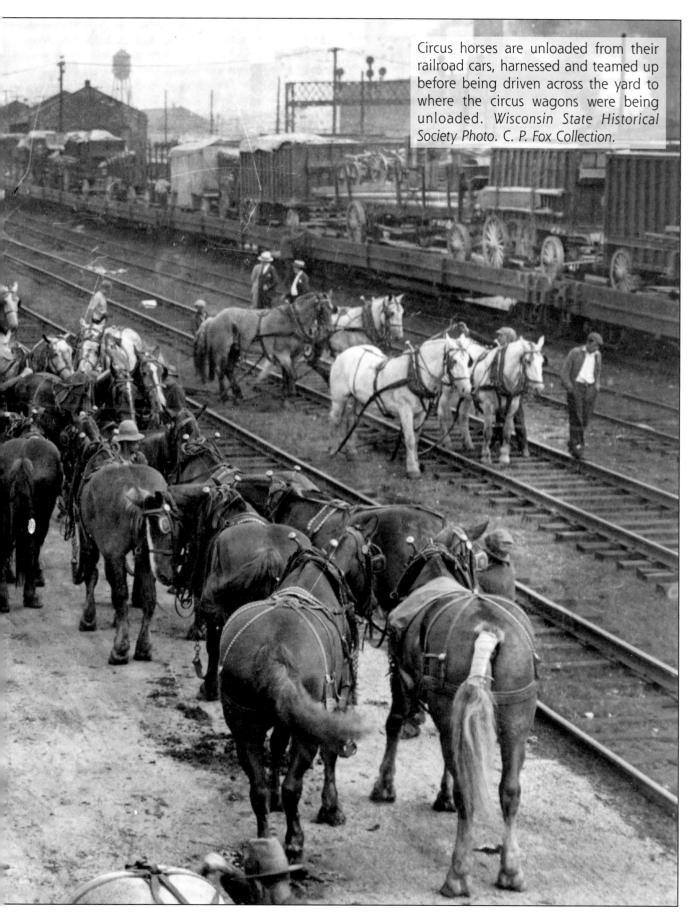

Circus horses are unloaded from their railroad cars, harnessed and teamed up before being driven across the yard to where the circus wagons were being unloaded. *Wisconsin State Historical Society Photo. C. P. Fox Collection.*

They Did It With Horses

Top: A circus parade on the streets of Louisville, Kentucky in 1910. *Bob Taber Collection.*
Bottom: A bandwagon pulled by six Percherons, date and place unknown. *Author's Collection.*

Chapter 7-Circus Horses

These photos are of two different units in the same circus parade taken from the same vantage point. Notice the children congregating as they walk beside the steam calliope in the bottom photo. *Harry Simpson Collection.*

They Did It With Horses

146

Chapter 7-Circus Horses

Opposite Page Top: This pole wagon from an unidentified circus in the 1920s sunk deep into the soft turf on its way to the circus lot. *John Zweifel Collection.*

Opposite Page Center: "Hook Roping" involved hooking several teams to large rings located at strategic spots on wagons so the combined horsepower could pull the load through deep mud or up a steep grade. Here, the Ringling Brothers and Barnum & Bailey Circus horses are pulling a large pole wagon at a Texas fairgrounds. *C. P. Fox Collection.*

Opposite Page Bottom: The Ringling Brothers and Barnum & Bailey Circus hook roping a large pole wagon at a Texas fairgrounds. *C. P. Fox Collection.*

Below: An unidentified circus pulling a wagon uphill. *Author's Collection.*

Bottom: Deep ruts left by the wagon may be seen in this photo. *Author's Collection.*

They Did It With Horses

Chapter 7-Circus Horses

Left: A crowd gathered to watch this unidentified circus unload by the river. Teams are being assigned wagons as they roll off the last railroad car. *C. P. Fox Collection.*

Below: A Ringling Brothers and Barnum & Bailey superintendent enjoys a smoke while his horses enjoy their feed after being unloaded and harnessed at their latest stop, this time in Milwaukee. 1937. *Author's Collection.*

They Did It With Horses

Chapter 7-Circus Horses

Clockwise from top left: A photo of the Norris & Rowe circus taken in 1908; An unidentified bandwagon pulled by ten Percherons; the Hagenback Wallace circus in Cleveland in 1923; and the Ringling and Barnum & Bailey circus hippopotamus cage in Allentown, Pennsylvania. *Author's Collection Photos.*

They Did It With Horses

Chapter 7-Circus Horses

Clockwise from Top, Opposite Page: The Hagenbeck Wallace Circus in West Allis, WIsconsin, in 1932, *C. P. Fox Collection;* the U.S. Bandwagon of the Ringling Brothers and Barnum & Bailey Circus in 1917, *C. P. Fox Collection;* an unidentified circus on parade with a ten-horse hitch of Belgians; *Author's Collection;* a general purpose wagon of the Ringling Brothers and Barnum & Bailey Circus in 1938, *C. P. Fox Collection;* the Howes Great London Circus, *Author's Collection;* getting a wagon started for the Ringling Brothers and Barnum & Bailey Circus, 1937, *Author's Collection.*

153

They Did It With Horses

Chapter 7-Circus Horses

Left: A small group of boys gather by the Ringling Brothers and Barnum & Bailey Percherons in 1946. *C. P. Fox Photo.*

Below: A fire hose fills the tank of this Ringling Brothers and Barnum & Bailey water wagon in West Allis, Wisconsin, in 1933. *C. P. Fox Photo.*

They Did It With Horses

Chapter 7-Circus Horses

Clockwise from top left: A leapord wagon of the Al J. Barnes circus at Riverside, California, in 1917, *Bob Taber Photo*; teamsters for an unidentified circus pause and relax during a trip between the railroad yard and the circus lot, *Author's Collection*; Ringling Brothers and Barnum & Bailey horses eat from their tie-lines in 1915; *C.P. Fox Collection;* and the Al Barnes-Sells Floto circus used this large wagon to carry its hippo, *Bob Taber Photo*.

Eight: From Brewery to Bar

Chapter 8-From Brewery to Bar

This Leinenkugel Brewing Company delivery wagon delivered beer in Chippewa Falls, WIsconsin, in 1880. *Courtesy of John Leinenkugel.*

They Did It With Horses

Above: Breweries chose solid, handsome horses for their delivery hitches. The Ballantine Brewery of Newark, New Jersey, used these well-fitted Percherons in 1916. *Author's Collection.*

Right: The Emmerling Brewing Company of Johnstown, Pennsylvania, made the delivery rounds with this pair of nicely-groomed horses in 1912. *Author's Collection.*

Chapter 8-From Brewery to Bar

They Did It With Horses

Left: The Storz Brewing Company used horses when gasoline and rubber was scarce during WW II. *Storz Brewing Company.*

Right: The Tivoli Brewing Company drove these four Belgian geldings in Denver in 1949. *Author's Collection.*

Chapter 8-From Brewery to Bar

The Genesee Brewing Company of Rochester, New York, is well known for its 12 horse roan Belgian hitches. Instead of the usual Belgians, this painting depicts 12 Clydesdales hooked to their wagon. This may have been a plan that never materialized. *Genesee Brewing Company.*

Chapter 8-From Brewery to Bar

Left: The American Brewing Company stabled 25 horses in 1941 and operated a number of horse drawn beer wagons in the 40s. *Author's Collection.*

Below: The Schaefer Brewing Company delivered cases of bottled beer with this team and wagon in 1933 New York City as prohibition ended. *Author's Collection.*

165

They Did It With Horses

Chapter 8-From Brewery to Bar

During World War II, the Schlitz Brewing Company contributed to the war effort with its delivery wagons and horse teams. *Ontario Archives.*

They Did It With Horses

Chapter 8-From Brewery to Bar

Top Left: Lang's Brewery of Buffalo, New York, drove this hitch of Clydesdales in 1945 before selling the horses to Anheuser Busch. The wagon was built by Studebaker Brothers Wagon Works, Indianapolis. *Ontario Archives.*

Above: The Budweiser Clydesdales in 1983, celebrating their Golden Anniversary. *Anheuser Busch Archives.*

Left: The Anheuser Busch brewery in its early days. *Anheuser Busch Archives.*

Nine: Daily Deliveries

Chapter 9-Daily Deliveries

Eight mailmen and their horsedrawn units line up outside the Bucyrus, Ohio, post office. The man standing in the doorway is probably the local postmaster. *Steele Studio and Camera Center Photo.*

They Did It With Horses

A fast, athletic horse, combined with a light but sturdy vehicle, made rural mail delivery a possibility. This unit delivered mail in Mansfield, Ohio, in 1906. *Author's Collection.*

Chapter 9-Daily Deliveries

173

They Did It With Horses

Chapter 9-Daily Deliveries

This open rear-end wagon was very handy for this mail carrier. Chicago, 1916. *Author's Collection.*

They Did It With Horses

Chapter 9-Daily Deliveries

In 1942, The Chicago Sun put its gasoline-powered delivery trucks in storage and returned to horsedrawn wagons to support the American cause in World War II. The string of mostly Percherons pictured below left were trained at the Chicago Union Stockyards by the Willett Teaming Company which supplied the Sun with their horses. *Norman Coughlin Photos.*

177

They Did It With Horses

Above and Opposite Bottom: The Chicago Tribune replaced its trucks with horses and delivery wagons during World War II. *Norman Coughlin Collection.*

Opposite Top: A load of newsprint being delivered to the Daily News in 1910. *Author's Collection.*

Chapter 9-Daily Deliveries

179

They Did It With Horses

Chapter 9-Daily Deliveries

Above: A Morgan gelding with a small handy ice delivery wagon. *Author's Collection.*

Left: A sturdy team of horses stands on a durable cobblestone street in 1904 Detroit. *Joseph Klima Photo.*

They Did It With Horses

Above: These two men, ice tongs in their hands, delivered ice to Chicago residents on the citiy's southwest side in 1907. *Norman Coughlin Collection.*

Right: No electric refrigerators, but how about a block of ice? This delivery man has his tongs slung over his shoulder. *Author's Collection.*

Chapter 9-Daily Deliveries

They Did It With Horses

Far Right: An express driver and his horse pause during the course of a day's work in Memphis, Tennessee, in 1910. *Author's Collection.*

Right: Blanketed horses on a cold morning before starting out for the day. The horses were docked at an angle to avoid blocking the roadway. 1914. *Smithsonian Institution.*

Below: The Adams Express Company had many rigs like this on the streets every day. The building in the background is the company's stable. Harrisburg, Pennsylvania, 1916. *Author's Collection.*

Chapter 9-Daily Deliveries

Hot-Weather Rules

Prepared By

The Boston Work-Horse Relief Association, 15 Beacon St.

1. Water your horse as often as possible. So long as a horse is working, water *in small quantities* will not hurt him. But let him drink only a few swallows if he is going to stand still. Do not fail to water him at night *after* he has eaten his hay.

2. When he comes in after work, sponge off the harness marks and sweat, his eyes, his nose and mouth, and the dock. Wash his feet but *not* his legs.

3. If the thermometer is 75 degrees or higher, wipe him all over with a *damp* sponge, using vinegar water if possible. Do *not* wash the horse at night.

4. Saturday night, give a bran mash lukewarm; and add a tablespoonful of saltpetre.

5. A sponge on top of the head, or even a cloth, is good if kept wet. If dry, it is worse than nothing.

6. If the horse is overcome by heat, get him into the shade, remove harness and bridle, wash out his mouth, sponge him all over, shower his legs, and give him two ounces of aromatic spirits of ammonia, or two ounces of sweet spirits of nitre, in a pint of water; or give him a pint of coffee, warm. Cool his head at once, using cold water, or, if necessary, chopped ice, wrapped in a cloth.

7. If the horse is off his feed, try him with two quarts of oats mixed with bran, and a little water, and add a little salt or sugar. Or give him oatmeal gruel or barley water to drink.

8. Watch your horse. If he stops sweating suddenly, or if he breathes short and quick, or if his ears droop, or if he stands with his legs braced sideways, he is in danger of a heat or sun stroke and needs attention at once.

9. If it is so hot that the horse sweats in the stable at night, *tie him outside*, with bedding under him. Unless he cools off during the night, he cannot well stand the next day's heat.

Chapter 9-Daily Deliveries

Left: An excellent specimen of horsepower. This horse is ideally suited for its work. *Author's Collection.*

Below: As pretty as a picture, an American Express Company outfit, fine horses, shiny harness, and a tip-top wagon they can be proud of. 1918. *American Railway Express Co.*

187

They Did It With Horses

A very sturdy outfit capable of delivering its load reliably and expeditously. *Smithsonian Institution.*

Chapter 9-Daily Deliveries

189

They Did It With Horses

Right: The fine conformation of this Percheron team ensured many yhears of service. These tank wagons generally held between 300 and 1000 gallons of petroleum or kerosene and used heavy platform or truck springs to carry the heavy load. 1916. *Author's Collection.*

Below Right: It took one horse and two mules to pull this very large tank wagon used by the Standard Oil Company in 1906. Hanging on the side of the wagon are the three nosebags and water bucket for feeding time later in the day. *Author's Collection.*

Chapter 9-Daily Deliveries

They Did It With Horses

Right: This photo shows how the tank wagons usually worked. The tank itself would be divided into sections, each containing a different type of fuel. The driver operated a faucet at the back of the wagon to dispense the fuel into his can which he carried to his customer's oil tank. This wagon was used at the former Amityville Mobilgas bulk plant in 1912. Abram Wanser, pictured in the photo, drove for the Mobilgas Company from 1906 until 1938. *Mobil Oil Corporation Photo.*

Below: Joseph and Sam Salamon with their oil and gasoline delivery rig in 1910. The two men eventually formed the Keystone Oil Supply and operated one of Cleveland's first gasoline stations. *Author's Collection.*

Chapter 9-Daily Deliveries

They Did It With Horses

Above: This wagon was pulled by a well-built Percheron and apparently guarded by a dog. Washington, D.C., 1916. *Norman Coughlin Collection.*

Right: This laundry business in Meadville, Pennsylvania, was owned and run by one family, providing personal service including delivery. *Author's Collection.*

Chapter 9-Daily Deliveries

They Did It With Horses

A Steinway piano being delivered in Cleveland, Ohio, in 1914. *Cleveland Public Library Archives.*

This medicine wagon was driven around Buffalo, New York, circa 1900. *Ontario Archives.*

Chapter 9-Daily Deliveries

Swanks Department Store of Johnstown, Pennsylvania, preferred black horses for their deliveries. 1902. *Author's Collection.*

They Did It With Horses

An Oscar Mayer hot dog wagon. *Author's Collection.*

Rye bread and sausage was delivered in this wagon in Milwaukee in 1909. *Norman Coughlin Collection.*

Chapter 9-Daily Deliveries

Personal service—you can't beat it. A delivery man talks to the lady of the house. *Author's Collection.*

The Fleischmann Yeast Company delivered their product with wagons like these in cities throughout the U.S. and Canada. 1916. *Author's Collection.*

Another Fleischmann Yeast Co. Wagon. 1920. *Author's Collection.*

Chapter 9-Daily Deliveries

Red Star deliverd with this turnout in Milwaukee in 1915. *Norman Coughlin Collection.*

Here a team pulled a larger yeast wagon in New York in 1900. *Author's Collection.*

201

Simpson's Department Store of Toronto, Canada, used gray or white horses to pull their delivery wagons. 1923. *Author's Collection.*

This fine, rubber-tired delivery wagon served its customers in 1916 Cleveland for the Halle Brothers Company department store. The teamster wore a coat, tie and derby. His assistant wore a coat, bow-tie and cap. *Herb Rebman Photo.*

Chapter 9-Daily Deliveries

The May Co. department store offered free delivery in Cleveland in 1921. *Author's Collection.*

This laundry delivered to homes and various businesses in 1914 Cleveland. *Author's Collection.*

They Did It With Horses

Chapter 9-Daily Deliveries

Top Left: A butcher works from his horsedrawn van on a road near Vulcan, Alberta, in 1910. *The Glenbow Institute.*

Bottom Left: A dry goods salesman pauses for a photo in Cleveland, circa 1915. *Author's Collection.*

Above: A publicity photo taken of a thriving butcher shop in downtown Elyria, Ohio, in 1887. *Author's Collection.*

Ten: Agriculture

Chapter 10-Agriculture

This combining crew worked a wheat field outside Colfax, Washington, in 1916, with sixteen horses, mostly Percheron, and a crew of four dusty men. *Spokane Chamber of Commerce Photo.*

They Did It With Horses

Chapter 10-Agriculture

Left: Good horses, good wagons, and good roads in 1912 rural Illinois. *John Deere Archives.*

Below: A powerful and solid team ready for a long day's work. *Cook & Gormley Photo.*

209

They Did It With Horses

In the 1920s, agriculture trade journals, horse associations, and universities emphasized larger hitches on America's farms to keep up with growing demand for grain. This crowd attended a plowing demonstration in Ohio in 1926. Notice that the men dressed in their Sunday best. *The Ohio Farmer.*

Chapter 10-Agriculture

They Did It With Horses

Four strong horses and a sharp, shiny plow on a midwestern farm in 1916. *Author's Collection.*

From the look of the horses' well-groomed manes, tails and coats, and flynets, this man cared deeply for his horses. 1912. *Author's Collection.*

Chapter 10-Agriculture

A Knox County, Ohio, team pulling a hay rack wagon on a farm lane in 1942. *Soil Conservation Service.*

They Did It With Horses

This 33-mule hitch was typical of those used in the American northwest in the early 1900s. The driver sat on a high perch and drove the hitch with just two lines running to the outside mules in the lead. *John Deere Photo.*

Chapter 10-Agriculture

They Did It With Horses

Chapter 10-Agriculture

Left: Good soil, a team of well-conditioned horses, and an experienced teamster showing how to plow nice straight furrows. *Author's Collection.*

Below: A Kingston, Ohio, farmer cultivating with four Belgian horses. *Author's Collection.*

They Did It With Horses

Above: A pair of mules provided the power for this hay loading operation in rural Indiana. *J.C. Allen Photo.*

Right: You can almost smell the hay being mowed by this Illinois farmer and his team in 1932. *John Deere Photo.*

Below: This team of horses worked together but far apart on this hay sweep. *Author's Collection.*

Chapter 10-Agriculture

They Did It With Horses

Above: An unusual, homemade fifth-wheel wagon with shafts hauling what is probably feed and water to livestock at a remote part of the farm. *Author's Collection.*

Right: A pair of quality dappled gray Percherons are hooked to a sled loaded with feed in rural Quebec in 1912.

Top RIght: The horses circling around this horsepower, powered a grinder in this 1896 photograph. *Milwaukee County Historical Society.*

Chapter 10-Agriculture

They Did It With Horses

Bigger hitches and more plows meant more land tilled per day by one man. This nine-horse hitch is pulling a single bottom sulky plow with another implement (perhaps another plow) hooked behind, out of the photo. 1926. *Horse and Mule Association of America.*

Chapter 10-Agriculture

A farmer and four horses with a grain binder opens up a field of wheat in Indiana in 1939. *Author's Collection.*

They Did It With Horses

Top: The horses are standing outside of the barn in readiness of the days' work. Kansas, Missouri, 1884. *Author's Collection.*

Bottom: This Belgian mare farm team competed at the 1917 Iowa State Fair. *Author's Collection.*

Chapter 10-Agriculture

Top: Four horses plowed a wheat field in 1910. *State Historical Society of North Dakota.*
Bottom: A team of grade horses on a grain drill in 1948. British Columbia. *Canadian Pacific Railroad Collection.*

225

They Did It With Horses

Chapter 10-Agriculture

Above: A dapple gray team competes at a plowing match in 1948. *British Percheron Association.*

Opposite Page: These combines were used extensively in the wheat fields of Washington and Oregon states. The crew included one or two men to bag the grain, a man to drive the horses or mules, and another man to adjust the angle of the beaters and to level the combine. The downhill wheels on the combine were cranked up and down to keep the machine level in hilly country like this. *Author's Collection.*

Eleven: Public Performance

Chapter 11-Public Performance

The champion six-horse-hitches and halter entries line up and parade for the audience at the 1948 Chicago International Livestock Show. Among the top hitch entries of the day were Anheuser Busch, Hawthorn Melody, Meadow Brook, Bob Jones and Wilson & Co. *Author's Collection.*

They Did It With Horses

This hitch of eight Belgian geldings was exhibited at the Santa Anita race track in California and owned by Dewey Burden. They are being driven in both photos by Harry Ogden. 1947.
Above: Frashers, Inc. Photo.
Right: Elmer G. Dyer Photo.

Chapter 11-Public Performance

They Did It With Horses

The White-O-Ranch of Healdsburg, California, was owned by Osborne and Aileen White and competed with both black and gray Percherons in the mid 1930s. *Abernathy Phtoto.*

Chapter 11-Public Performance

Above Top: A rube band performing in a 1929 Chardon, Ohio, parade. *Author's Collection.*

Above Bottom: Hitches like this one, the Percherons of the Chestnut Farms Dairy, served as public relations tools as they competed before large audiences at shows throughout America. *Abernathy Photo.*

They Did It With Horses

The Wilson and Co. Clydesdale Hitch taking a practice drive in 1936 Chicago. *Kaufmann & Fabry Photo.*

Chapter 11-Public Performance

Top: The Wilson & Co. hitch of Clydesdales photographed in Pensacola, Florida. *Author's Collection.*

Center: The Babson Farms hitched these six Shires in the early 1920s. *Abernathy Photo.*

Bottom: The highly regarded Chicago Union Stockyard Clydesdale hitch in front of the famous Stockyard Inn in 1935. *Norman Coughlin Photo.*

They Did It With Horses

Inset: Bob Anguish owned and drove this team of Percherons at an Ohio county fair in 1978. Author Philip Weber is his passenger. *Bob Smith Photo.*

Right: The O'Keefe Brewing Company of Toronto, Canada, hitched these Clydesdales at the Ottowa Exhibition. *Author's Collection.*

Chapter 11-Public Performance

237

Top: A Belgian team owned by Charles Wentz of Kirby, Ohio, placed first at the 1929 Ohio State Fair. *Author's Collection.*

Bottom: The Sweet Briar entry at the 1928 Chicago International, George Miller driving. *Author's Collection.*

Chapter 11-Public Performance

Top: The Honsberger family of northwestern Ohio have been showing their Percherons since the 1950s. *Lloyd W Goon Photo.*

Bottom: L.B. Wescott of Clinton, New Jersey, was one of the leading promoters of Suffolk horses. With a team like this it is easy to understand why. *Photo Courtesy of L.B. Wescott.*

They Did It With Horses

Chapter 11-Public Performance

Top Left: A group of girls on a float in the 1912 Calgary Stampede parade. *Glenbow Foundation Photo.*

Left: This Clydesdale hitch was owned by Nelson Morris and Company of Chicago and was one of the earliest and best big show hitches. *Huber Gillaugh Collection.*

Below: The Eshelman Feed Company pulled this large heavy wagon and load in 1946 with their six horse hitch of Belgians. *Robert D. Good Photo.*

They Did It With Horses

Lloyd Jentes operated the Lazy J Ranch in Wooster, Ohio, a recreational facility. An all-around horseman, Jentes is shown performing at the 1950 Wooster Fair. *Author's Collection.*

Chapter 11-Public Performance

They Did It With Horses

Renowned horseman Harold Clark worked for the Meadowbrook Farm in Rochester, Michigan, from 1942 until 1973. He is shown driving in 1943 and judging at the 1956 Indiana State Fair. *Author's Collection (above) and Indiana State Fair Photo (inset).*

Chapter 11-Public Performance

245

They Did It With Horses

A team of Percherons pulling a dynamometer in a lightweight draft class in 1926. *Horse & Mule Association of America.*

Chapter 11-Public Performance

247

Twelve: Street Scenes

Chapter 12-Street Scenes

By-Ward Market, York Street, Ottawa, Ontario, circa 1905. *Public Archives of Canada.*

They Did It With Horses

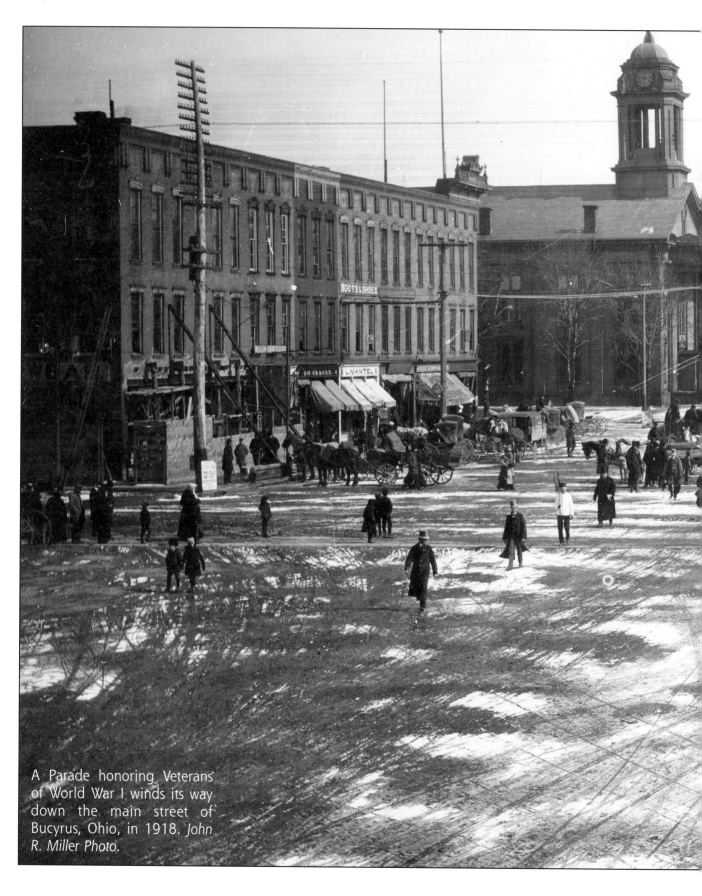

A Parade honoring Veterans of World War I winds its way down the main street of Bucyrus, Ohio, in 1918. *John R. Miller Photo.*

Chapter 12-Street Scenes

They Did It With Horses

Top: A busy scene of south Water Street in Chicago, Illinois, 1920. *Author's Collection*
Bottom: The intersection of Dearborn and Randolph streets in 1900 Chicago. *Author's Collection*

Chapter 12-Street Scenes

Top: City Market in Meadville, Pennsylvania, undated. *Author's Collection*
Bottom: South Water Street, Chicago. 1910. *Author's Collection*

They Did It With Horses

Chapter 12-Street Scenes

Left Top: State Street, Chicago, 1908. *Author's Collection.*
Left Center: Main Street, Warrenton, Virginia, undated. *Author's Collection.*
Left Bottom: Market Street, San Francisco, 1889. *Author's Collection.*
Above: Faneuil Hall, Boston, undated. *Author's Collection.*